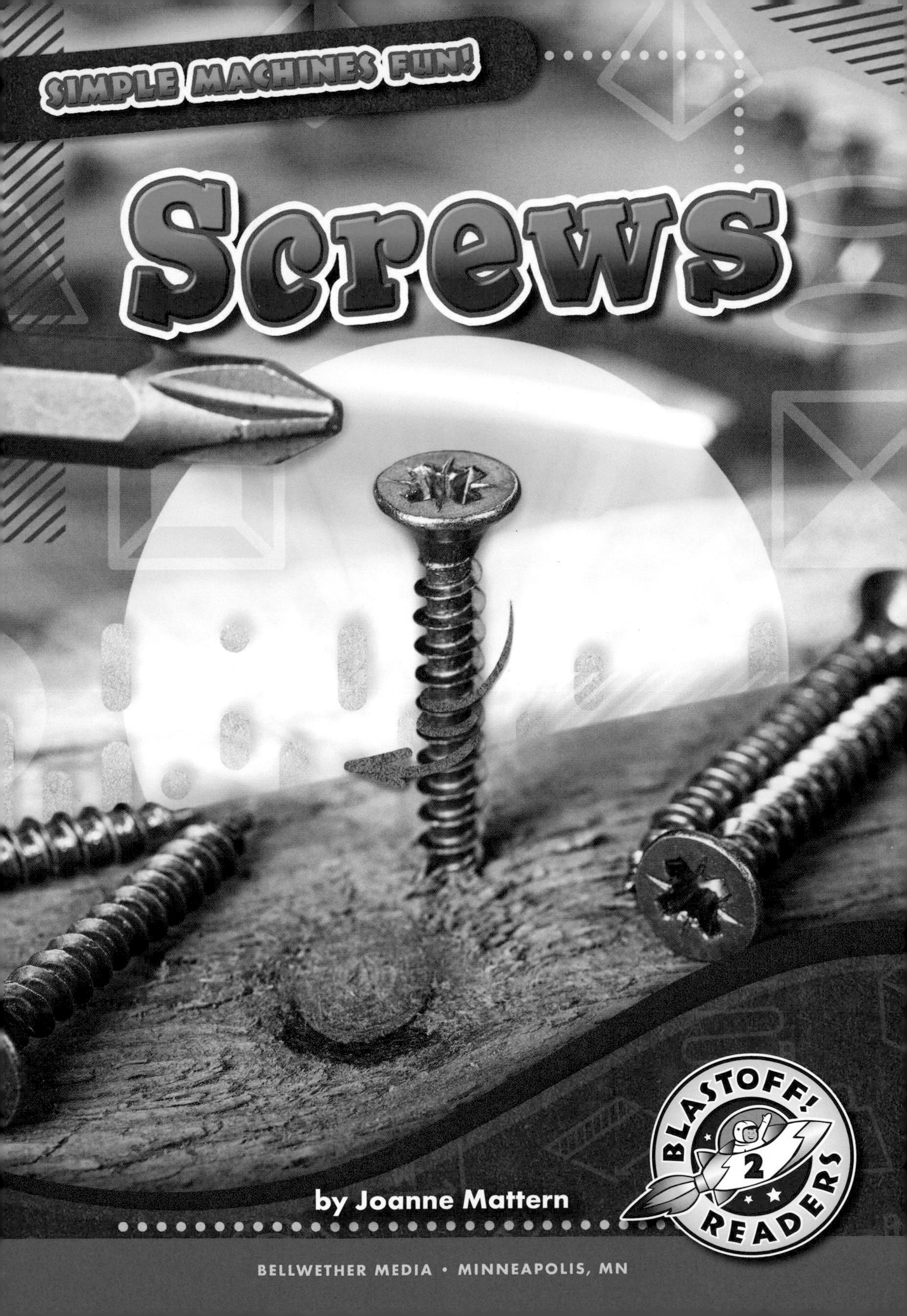
SIMPLE MACHINES FUN!
Screws
by Joanne Mattern
BLASTOFF! 2 READERS
BELLWETHER MEDIA • MINNEAPOLIS, MN

Note to Librarians, Teachers, and Parents:

Blastoff! Readers are carefully developed by literacy experts and combine standards-based content with developmentally appropriate text.

Level 1 provides the most support through repetition of high-frequency words, light text, predictable sentence patterns, and strong visual support.

Level 2 offers early readers a bit more challenge through varied simple sentences, increased text load, and less repetition of high-frequency words.

Level 3 advances early-fluent readers toward fluency through increased text and concept load, less reliance on visuals, longer sentences, and more literary language.

Level 4 builds reading stamina by providing more text per page, increased use of punctuation, greater variation in sentence patterns, and increasingly challenging vocabulary.

Level 5 encourages children to move from "learning to read" to "reading to learn" by providing even more text, varied writing styles, and less familiar topics.

Whichever book is right for your reader, Blastoff! Readers are the perfect books to build confidence and encourage a love of reading that will last a lifetime!

This edition first published in 2020 by Bellwether Media, Inc.

Library of Congress Cataloging-in-Publication Data

Names: Mattern, Joanne, 1963- author.
Title: Screws / by Joanne Mattern.
Description: Minneapolis, MN : Bellwether Media, Inc., 2020. | Series: Blastoff! Readers: Simple Machines Fun! | Includes bibliographical references and index. | Audience: 5-8. | Audience: K to grade 3.
Identifiers: LCCN 2018056035 (print) | LCCN 2018060220 (ebook) | ISBN 9781618915344 (ebook) | ISBN 9781626179943 (hardcover : alk. paper)
Subjects: LCSH: Screws--Juvenile literature.
Classification: LCC TJ1338 (ebook) | LCC TJ1338 .M329 2020 (print) | DDC 621.8/82--dc23
LC record available at https://lccn.loc.gov/2018056035

Editor: Christina Leaf Designer: Jeffrey Kollock

Printed in the United States of America, North Mankato, MN.

Table of Contents

What Are Screws?

Have you ever seen a spiral staircase? It is a simple machine called a screw.

Screws raise or lower things by turning them.

Screws can also hold things together. Screws **connect** two pieces of wood.

They hold lids on jars.

A screw is an **inclined plane** with a twist. A **thread** wraps around a rod.

Because it moves in a circle, a screw takes up less space than an inclined plane.

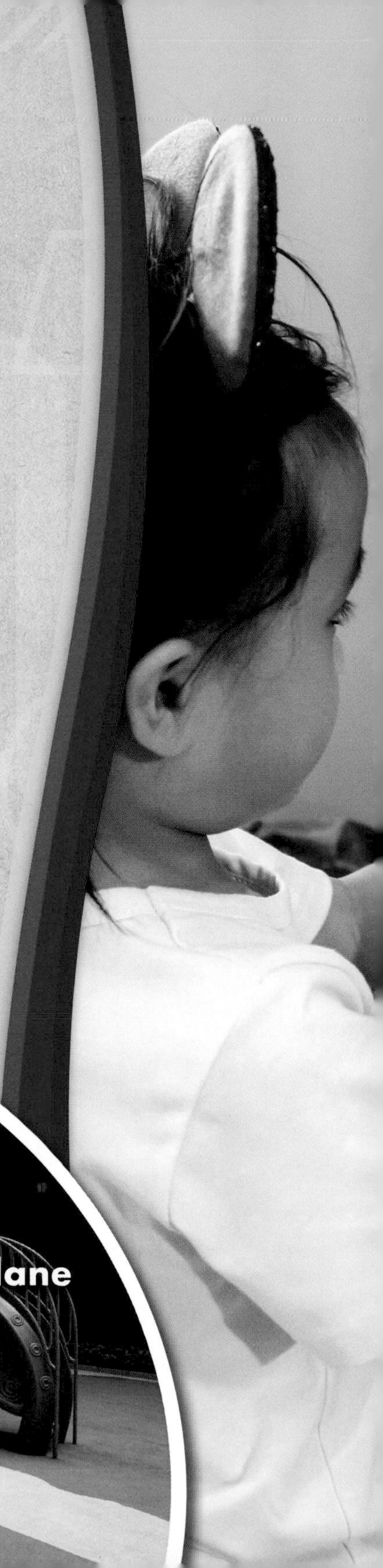

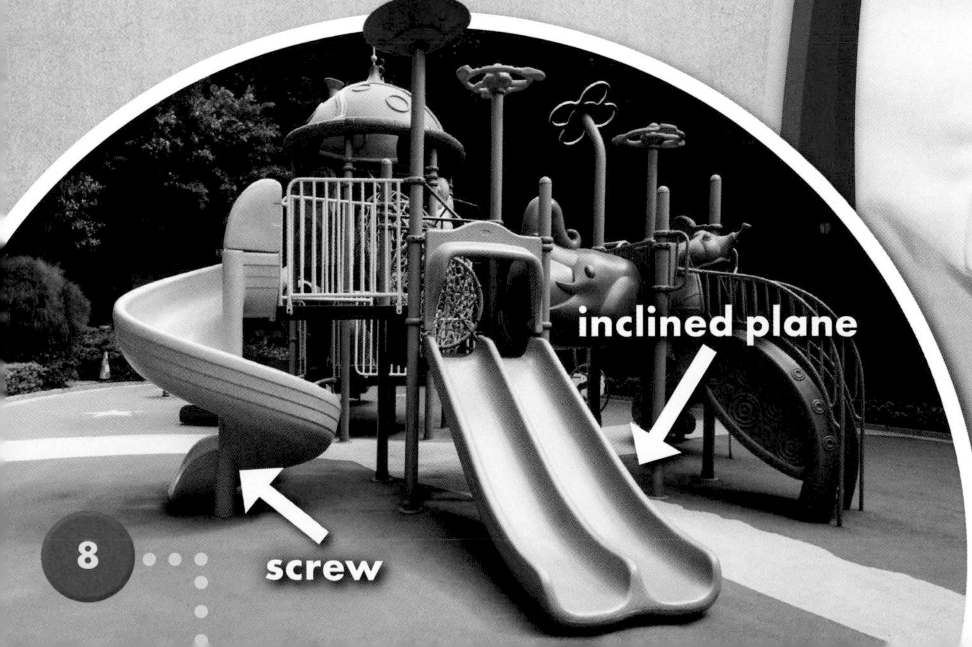

inclined plane

screw

thread

How Do Screws Work?

Screws turn **rotational force** into **linear motion**. When the screw turns, the thread pulls it forward.

This **force** moves the screw up or down.

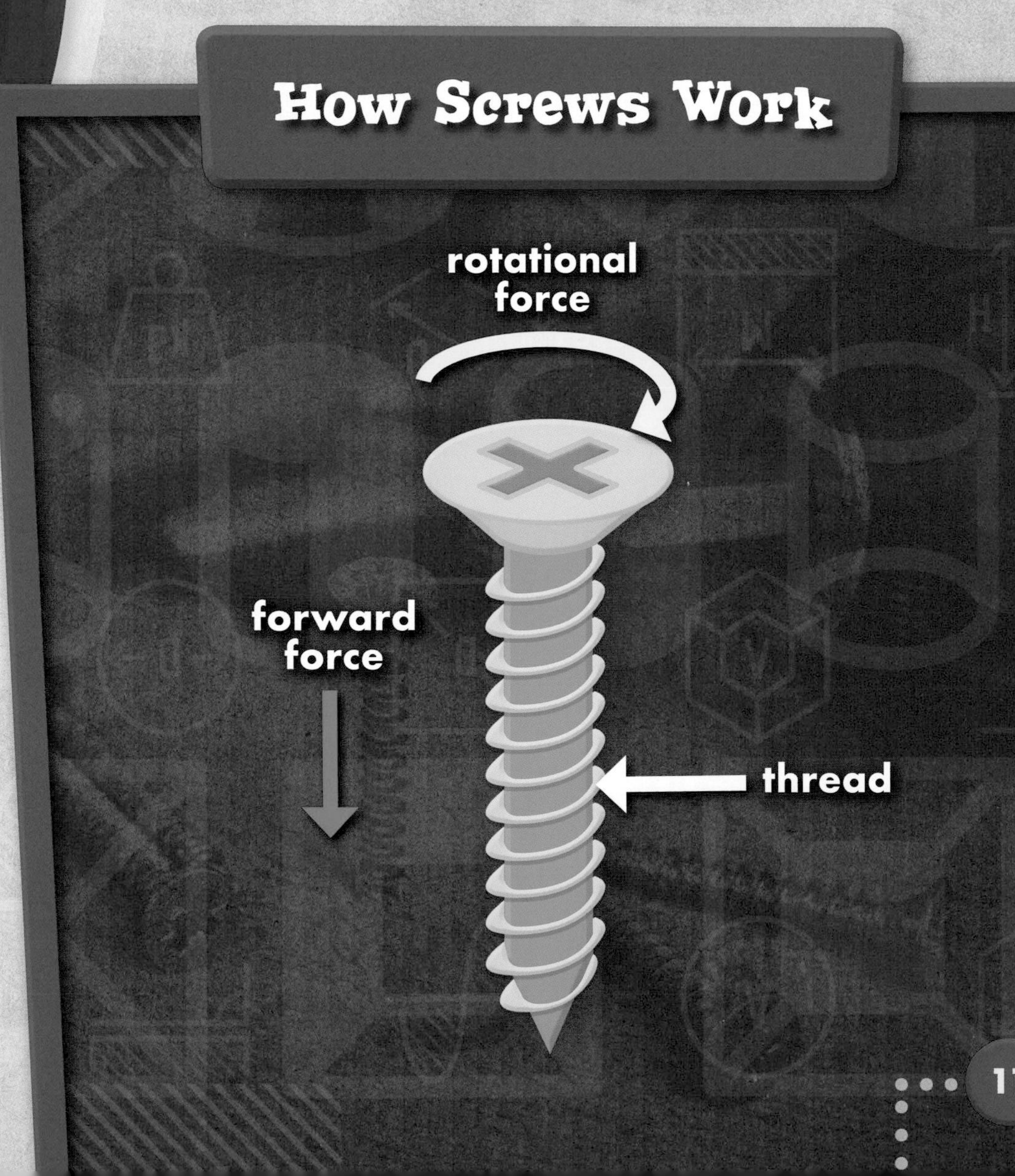

Thread Distance

What You Need:

- scrap wood
- coarse screws, with threads that are far apart
- fine screws, with threads that are close together
- a screwdriver

What To Do:

1. Try to push the screws into the wood without turning them. It is hard to do!
2. Use a screwdriver to screw some of the fine screws into the wood.
3. Next, use a screwdriver to screw some of the coarse screws into the wood.
4. Which screw is easier to use? Why do you think that is?

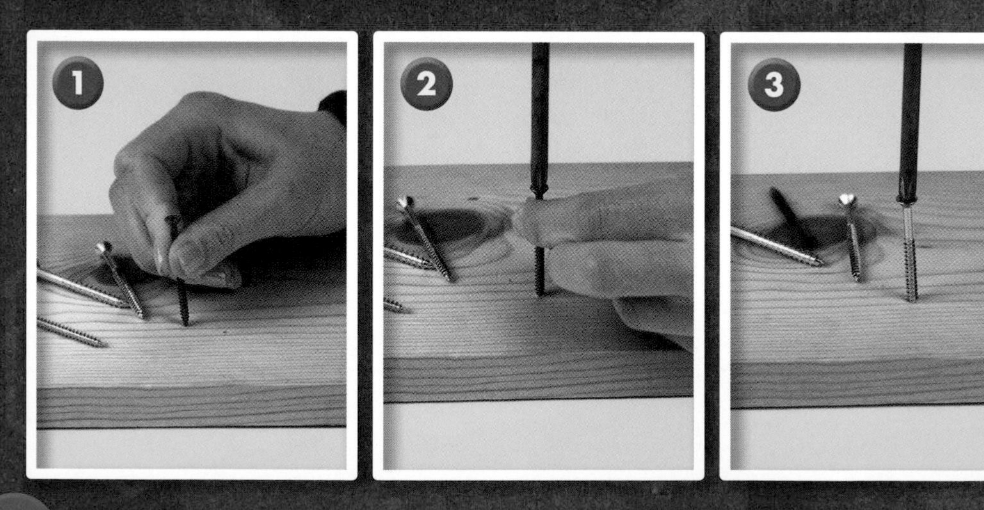

Some screws have threads that are close together. Some threads are far apart. Far apart threads need more force.

Turning a screw can be hard. Sometimes a **motor** turns the screw.

A large motor and a long screw can do a big job!

Screws in Our Lives

Archimedes screw

Long ago, a man named Archimedes used a screw to lift water. Today, we still use screws to drive pumps.

Archimedes Screw

What You Need:

- two bowls
- clear packing tape
- food coloring
- water
- clear plastic tubing, 1/4-inch diameter
- a piece of PVC pipe or another long cylinder that can go in water

What To Do:

1. Wrap the clear tubing around the pipe and tape it in place. Now you have a screw!
2. Pour some water in one bowl. Add a few drops of food coloring.
3. Place one end of your screw into the bowl of water at an angle. Place a bowl under the other end to catch the water.
4. Turn the screw. Watch the water run up the tube and into the bowl!

We use screws in many ways. Handles on faucets turn screws to let water flow.

On farms, screws help lift grain into **silos**.

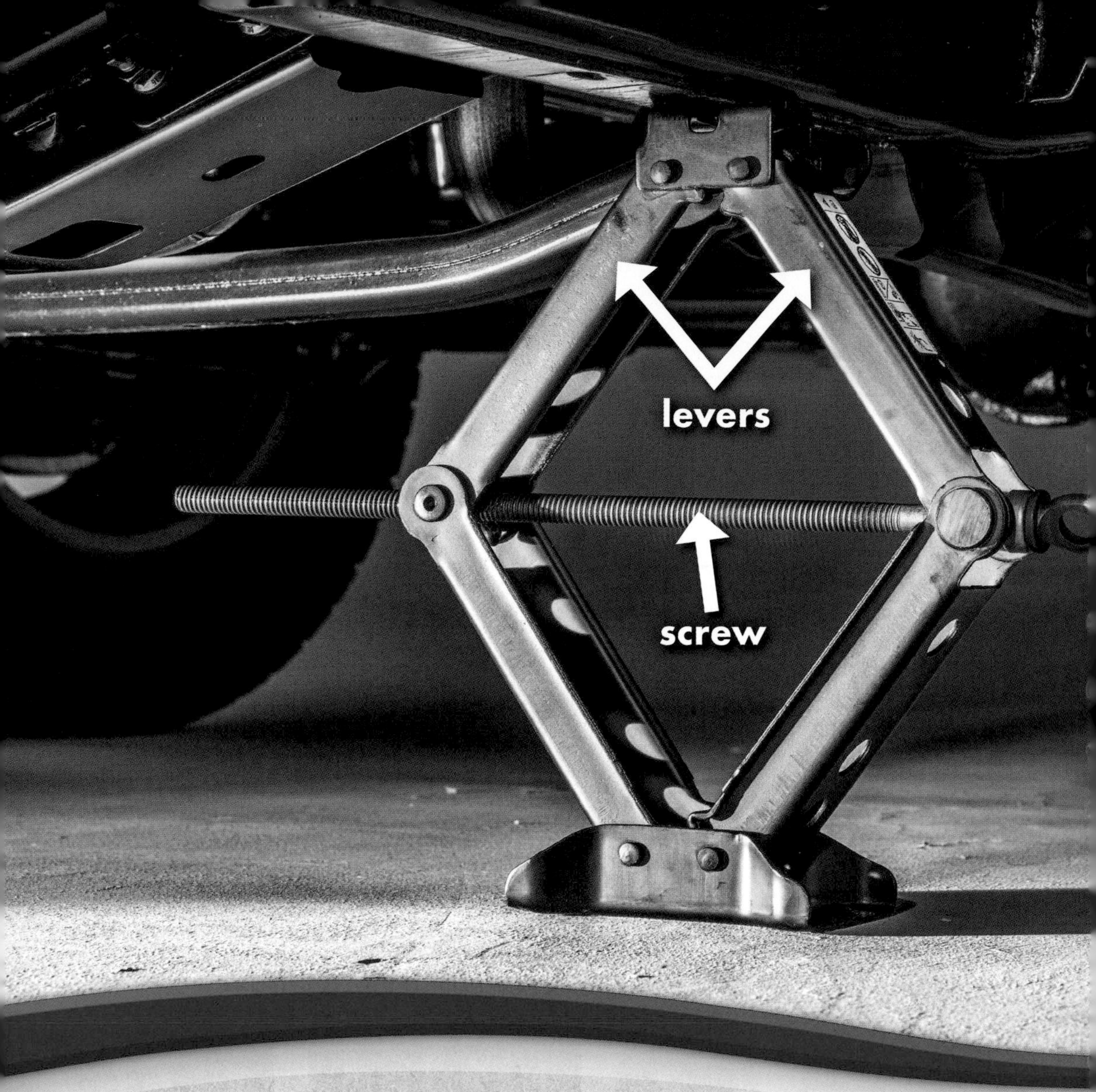

A car jack is a **complex machine**. A person turns a screw inside the jack. The screw lifts the **levers**, which lift the car.

Everyday Screws

Simple

light bulbs

bottle caps

Complex

drills

faucets

The turn of a screw can do so much work!

Glossary

complex machine—a machine that combines two or more simple machines

connect—to hold things together

force—energy that has an effect on something

inclined plane—a simple machine with one end that is higher than the other

levers—simple machines that turn on a point to help with lifting

linear motion—motion in a straight line

motor—a machine powered by an engine

rotational force—energy created by turning an object around a fixed point

silos—tall bins on farms that store grains and other crops

thread—a ridge on the outside of a screw

To Learn More

AT THE LIBRARY

Dickmann, Nancy. *Screws.* Tucson, Ariz.: Brown Bear Books, 2018.

Oxlade, Chris. *Making Machines with Screws.* Chicago, Ill.: Heinemann Raintree, 2015.

Rivera, Andrea. *Screws.* Minneapolis, Minn.: Abdo Zoom, 2017.

ON THE WEB

FACTSURFER

Factsurfer.com gives you a safe, fun way to find more information.

1. Go to www.factsurfer.com.

2. Enter "screws" into the search box and click 🔍.

3. Select your book cover to see a list of related web sites.

Index

The images in this book are reproduced through the courtesy of: Kucher Serhii, front cover; Ciovanni Cardilo, pp. 4-5; miljko, p. 5; Michal Bellan, p. 6; real444, pp. 6-7; hxdbzxy, p. 8; v74, pp. 8-9; schankz, pp. 10-11; Bellwether Media, pp. 12 (all), 17; domnitsky, p. 13; il21, p. 14; Dmitry Kalinovsky, pp. 14-15; Nor Gal, p. 16; Jeff Baumgart, p. 18; Earl D. Walker, pp. 18-19; Nidvoray, p. 19; Kenny CMK, pp. 20-21; patpitchaya, p. 21 (light bulbs); Jiri Vacalvek, p. 21 (bottle caps); Rido, p. 21 (drill); InnaFelker, p. 21 (faucet).